UNCOVERING HISTORY
ANCIENT GREECE

First published in 2001 by McRae Books
Copyright © 2001 McRae Books Srl, Florence (Italy)

Everyday Life in Ancient Greece
was created and produced by McRae Books
Borgo Santa Croce, 8 – Florence (Italy)
e-mail: mcrae@tin.it

SERIES EDITOR Anne McRae
TEXT Cath Senker
ILLUSTRATIONS Manuela
Cappon, Luisa Della Porta,
Lorenzo Cecchi, Matteo
Chesi, Giuliano Fornari, Studio
Inklink, Paola Ravaglia, Studio
Stalio (Alessandro Cantucci,
Fabiano Fabbrucci, Andrea Morandi)
GRAPHIC DESIGN Marco Nardi
LAYOUT Laura Ottina, Adriano Nardi
EDITING Susan Kelly, Vicky Egan
REPRO Litocolor, Florence
PICTURE RESEARCH Susan Kelly

Published in the United States by Smart Apple Media
1980 Lookout Drive, North Mankato, Minnesota 56003

Printed and bound in Italy

Library of Congress Cataloging-in-Publication Data
Senker, Cath.
Everyday life in ancient Greece / Cath Senker; illustrations by
Manuela Cappon, Luisa Della Porta, Paola Ravaglia, Studio Stalio.
p. cm. — (Uncovering history)
Summary: A brief, illustrated overview of the geography, history,
customs, beliefs, monuments, day-to-day life, and social structure
of ancient Greece, a civilization that flourished for almost 2,000
years.
ISBN 1-58340-248-9
1. Greece—Social life and customs—Juvenile literature. [1.
Greece—Social life and customs—To 146 B.C. 2. Greece—
Civilization—To 146 B.C.] I. Title: Ancient Greece. II. Title. III.
Series.

DF78 .S46 2003
938—dc21   2002036611

First Edition
9 8 7 6 5 4 3 2

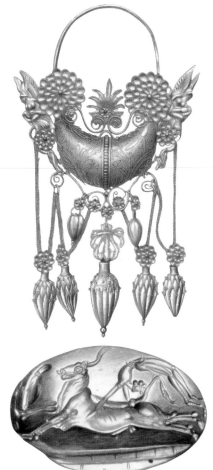

Cath Senker

ANCIENT
EVERYDAY LIFE IN
GREECE

Illustrations by Manuela Cappon, Luisa Della Porta,
Paola Ravaglia, Studio Stalio

Smart Apple Media

Table of Contents

Introduction

The ancient Greeks lived 2,000 years ago, but their legacy lives on. In our everyday lives today, we can spot Greek influence in our language, medical practices, scientific work, and political systems—not to mention architecture, poetry, philosophy, and theater. Our alphabet, for example, was adapted from that of the ancient Greeks, and many of our words have Greek roots. The word "alphabet" itself comes from the words *alpha* and *beta*, the first two letters of the Greek alphabet. And the word "telephone" comes from the Greek word *tele* (far off) and *phone* (voice). Today, doctors have to follow a strict code of practice that has its roots in the methods of the ancient Greek doctor Hippocrates. They still swear the "Hippocratic Oath," in which they promise to do everything possible to benefit the patient. Other early Greek thinkers influenced science. They realized that natural events had natural causes, and were not simply the work of the gods. Today, we take it for granted that there are scientific reasons why the sun rises in the morning, why plants grow, and why violent storms occur. Many people today live in a democracy—by voting, they choose who they want to govern them. This idea started with the ancient Greeks, who allowed male citizens to vote for their political leaders. (Women and slaves were excluded, so the system was not truly democratic, but it was the start of modern democracy.) This book gives you a taste of what life was like for the ancient Greeks, and shows you how the lives and ideas of people who lived so long ago are linked to our own lives today.

Chronology of Ancient Greece

PELOPONNESE SETTLED BY EARLY GREEKS
2000 B.C.

MINOAN CIVILIZATION FLOURISHES ON CRETE
2000–1600 B.C.

MYCENEAN CIVILIZATION APPEARS IN SOUTHERN GREECE
1650 B.C.

GREEK "DARK AGES"
1220–900 B.C.

CITY-STATES EMERGE IN GREECE
c. 1100–500 B.C.

MAIN PERIOD OF GREEK COLONIZATION
c. 820–600 B.C.

PERSIAN WARS
510–449 B.C.

DEMOCRATIC GOVERNMENT ESTABLISHED IN ATHENS
507 B.C.

DELIAN LEAGUE SET UP
478 B.C.

THE CLASSICAL PERIOD
480–330 B.C.

HELLENIC LEAGUE OF GREEK STATES SET UP
340 B.C.

HELLENISTIC PERIOD
323–146 B.C.

Before the Greeks

Mainland Greece and the islands of the Aegean and Adriatic Seas make up the Greek world. The first civilizations developed in the region in the third millennium B.C. on the Cyclades Islands and on Crete, where the Minoans flourished. Then, about 1650 B.C., the Mycenean civilization emerged on the mainland. By 1200 B.C., these cultures had come to a violent end, and four centuries of poverty followed, known as the Greek "Dark Ages." Prosperity returned in the eighth century B.C., leading to the "Golden Age" in the fifth century B.C.

Above: The decoration on this gold ring shows a man vaulting over the back of a running bull. No one knows exactly why the Minoans practiced "bull-leaping," but the ritual seems to have had magical or religious significance. The bull was a sacred symbol to the Minoans.

The head of a Cycladic statue from Antiparos. The civilization of the Cyclades Islands flourished between 2200 and 1700 B.C., when the people of the islands built important settlements and prospered.

Right: A nine-inch-high (23 cm) terracotta model of a two-story Minoan villa. Inside, a tiny staircase leads to the second story. Columns support the flat roof, and there is a small balcony on one of the end walls.

The Minoans

The Minoans grew grapes, grain, and olives, and also raised livestock. They traded with other towns in Greece and around the Mediterranean, as well as with Egypt and Syria. After developing a form of picture writing, they created a writing system using symbols for the sounds that make up words.

Left: A Minoan bull's head rhyton—*a drinking vessel used in sacred ceremonies.*

Art and luxury items

Minoan artists produced beautiful sculptures and decorated the walls of their palaces on Crete with colorful frescoes of religious ceremonies, dancers, athletes, plants, and animals. Skilled craftspeople made pottery, jewelry, and metalwork for the rich. This highly decorated *krater* (left) was used at banquets for diluting wine with water. It was found in the Cretan palace of Phaistos.

Knossos

The palace at Knossos (left) was the largest Minoan palace on Crete. Built about 2000 B.C., it was constructed around a central courtyard and was several stories high. The ground floor and basements were used as store rooms and workshops. On the upper stories were royal apartments and other elaborately decorated living areas.

The flourishing Cretan harbor town of Gournia, about 1500 B.C. The women are selling the latest catch of fish, and two porters have just carried some precious ivory tusks up from the boats on the beach. Ivory was imported from Libya.

The Myceneans

The Myceneans lived in cities with strong, protective walls. A warrior people, they conquered Crete about 1450 B.C. They were great traders, selling pottery and farm products in Asia Minor, Egypt, Cyprus, and Italy in exchange for metals and ivory.

A gold funeral mask (c. 1500–1400 B.C.) from a Mycenean tomb. The Myceneans placed masks of this type on the faces of their kings when they died.

Right: A Mycenean stemmed bowl (c. 1400–1300 B.C.) from Cyprus. The horses are drawing light, two-wheeled chariots. In the Mycenean world, chariots were used by the army and also as part of spectacular parades.

Right: This Mycenean lion's head rhyton, from the 16th century B.C., was used in ritual ceremonies. Liquids were poured into it through one hole, and they flowed out through another.

9

Colonies

Prosperity returned to Greece in the eighth century B.C., but the growing population was unable to produce enough food from the country's poor, dry soils, and new food sources had to be found. Numerous expeditions set out to look for good land to colonize, and over the next 200 years, settlers built farming communities all along the Mediterranean and Black Sea coasts. Many of the colonies developed into trading posts, and some—such as Syracuse—became extremely wealthy. Successful colonies were able to send food to Greece when it had shortages.

An altar statue of the Medusa, from the Greek colony of Syracuse, Sicily. Founded in 734 B.C., the colony became one of the main ports of the western Mediterranean.

Early colonies

In the eighth century B.C., the Greeks established many colonies in Sicily and southern Italy. Young Greek men were sent by ship to found the colonies. Despite the possibility of gaining land and becoming rich, many were reluctant to make the long and dangerous sea journeys.

The leader of an expedition had to choose the best site for the new colony. Some colonists were welcomed by the native people; others had to fight for land.

Left: This "red-figure" vase of a soldier on horseback, painted by Euphronius in 500 B.C., was found in Italy. It suggests that Greek colonizers were not always welcomed with open arms by the local people, and sometimes had to use force to take power. Greek pots from the eighth century B.C. have been found at more than 80 sites outside the Greek homeland.

A statue of the nature goddess Cybele, who came originally from Asia before she was adopted by the Greeks. Believed to preside over mountains and fortresses, she was often depicted wearing a crown shaped like a city wall. She is seen here playing her drum.

A vase painting showing King Arkesilas of Cyrene (a Greek colony in Libya, founded about 631 B.C.). He is supervising the weighing and storage of herbs from North Africa. One of the main reasons for colonization was to provide more land to grow food crops.

Magna Grecia

From 770 B.C., the Greeks founded so many colonies along the coast of southern Italy—a region rich in natural harbors and good farmland—that the area became known as Magna Grecia, or Greater Greece. The colonies were independent of Greece, but the colonists continued to live, farm, and make goods in the Greek style, and the Greek civilization flourished there. Magna Grecia became a main center of trade and commerce.

Gods

Greek leaders always consulted the gods when they had important decisions to make. Before sending settlers to a new colony, they asked the god Apollo for his approval. The settlers took their religious beliefs to the lands they colonized and built temples to their gods in the new lands. But they also adopted gods from other cultures and worshiped them, sometimes in different forms in different places, all over the Greek world.

Greek merchants traded with northern Europe. This krater, or vase, for example, was made in Sparta in the sixth century B.C., but was found in a grave in central France. It is five feet (1.65 m) tall and weighs 458 pounds (208 kg)!

A map of the main Greek colonies and trade routes around the Mediterranean and Black Seas (800–500 B.C.).

Greek influence

The Greeks not only influenced the cultures of the places they colonized; they also had an influence on countries with whom they traded. The colonists spread the Greek language, lifestyle, and beliefs wherever they went, and also their craft skills. They, in turn, were influenced by the ways of life of the countries where they settled.

This earring (above) was found in ancient Scythia, one of the Black Sea colonies. It was probably made by a Greek jeweler who had been influenced by the Scythian style.

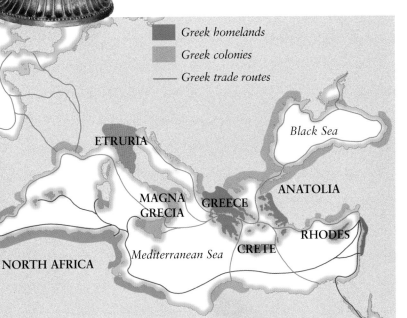

- Greek homelands
- Greek colonies
- Greek trade routes

SPAIN

ETRURIA

Black Sea

MAGNA GRECIA

GREECE

ANATOLIA

NORTH AFRICA

Mediterranean Sea

CRETE

RHODES

Society

In Greece, individual city-states with their own governments started to develop from the eighth century B.C. Often, city-states were ruled by an oligarchy, or small elite. At other times they were ruled by tyrants—men who seized power for themselves and ruled sometimes fairly, sometimes with great cruelty. Led by Athens, some city-states developed the political system called "democracy." Democracy means "rule by the people," but in fact only a minority of the people were eligible to govern. They had to be "citizens"—men who were born in the city. Women and slaves had no political rights.

A bronze statue of an African slave. Almost every household in Greece owned at least one slave.

Slaves

Slavery became widespread in Greece after 600 B.C. Most slaves had been captured as prisoners of war. They were made to work in the gold and silver mines, as household slaves, and in their masters' businesses. Slaves had no rights, but could sometimes buy their freedom.

Democracy

Athens established the world's first democracy in the sixth century B.C. The city was divided into 10 blocks, called tribes, which elected men to a council. The council carried out the daily work of government and raised issues or ideas for the Assembly to discuss.

Solon (left) helped make Athens more democratic. Elected as an archon, or ruler, in 594 B.C., he gave power to four new property-owning classes and allowed members of the highest three classes to hold government posts. He introduced rights of appeal into Greek law and forbade the selling of Athenians into slavery if they could not pay their debts.

A vase decoration showing Athenian citizens voting in the Assembly.

Citizens

Only one quarter of the people in Athens in the sixth century B.C. were citizens. Women, foreigners, slaves, and children under 18 were excluded. Only citizens could own property, go to festivals, or take part in the Assembly. Citizens who were slow to volunteer to go to the Assembly were marked as being lazy—they were hauled in by a rope that was dripping with red paint!

Women

Women's lives were controlled by their fathers or husbands. A girl was married at age 13 or 14 to an older man, who was chosen by her father. Wealthy women spent most of their time managing their households. Poor women usually worked outside the home as well, often selling goods in the market.

This woman is spinning wool into yarn. Spinning and weaving were women's work.

These two girls are playing knucklebones (a form of this game is still played by some children today). Girls in ancient Greece were thought less valuable than boys, and some were even abandoned at birth.

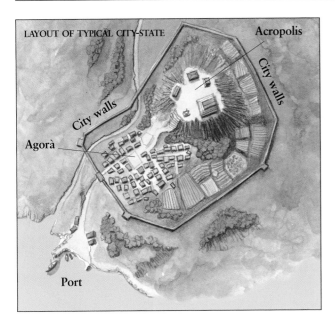

LAYOUT OF TYPICAL CITY-STATE

Acropolis

City walls

City walls

Agora

Port

Below: The citizens of Athens could vote to send an unpopular citizen into exile. The person's name was scratched onto an ostraca (a piece of pottery).

Ostracism

In mid-fifth-century Athens, high-ranking officials and generals were under pressure to perform well. If they were corrupt or failed in their duties, they could be ostracized—banned from the city-state. The 6,000 members of the Assembly voted by ballot for their least favorite person, and the man who was named the most times had to leave Athens for 10 years.

The *polis*

By 750 B.C., most of Greece was divided into several hundred *poleis*, or "city-states." The people of a city and its surrounding land made up a *polis*. Most city-states were built near a river or the sea. They had a wall to protect them. High on a hill was the *acropolis* (citadel), with its temples, and there was an *agora* (marketplace) nearby.

These citizens of the Assembly of Athens are making their way up the hill to the acropolis. The Assembly made laws and decided on important issues, such as whether to go to war. Ordinary citizens could attend to speak and vote. A minimum of 6,000 men had to be present for the meeting to take place.

Farming and Country Life

The ancient Greek economy was based on farming. Grapes and olives flourished on the hill slopes around the city, but the poor, stony soils made it hard for farmers to grow cereal crops. Fields were sown and harvested one year, and left bare, or fallow, the next, which allowed the soil to regain some fertility. But often there was not enough rain, and the crops died (the Greeks had to rely on imported grain from their colonies to survive). Country folk raised sheep, goats, and chickens, and kept bees for their honey.

Left: A terracotta relief of Persephone and Hades in the Underworld. Persephone and her mother, Demeter, were the goddesses of grain, whom the Greeks asked for good harvests. According to myth, Persephone spent two-thirds of the year on Earth—a time of plenty, when plants flourished and farmers grew and harvested their crops. When she returned to her husband, Hades, in the Underworld, the world was plunged into bitter winter.

Right: A statue of a god portrayed as a shepherd holding a lamb. Shepherds played a vital role because sheep were grazed at some distance from the city. With no fences around the fields, sheep were in constant danger from hungry wild animals.

The farming year

Farm work was done by hand, using simple tools and domestic animals. In October, farmers plowed the fields and planted barley and wheat. Grain crops grew during the winter, when the most rain fell. Harvest-time was in April or May. Then the fields were plowed once more and left empty so that the soil had time to become fertile again before new crops were planted in October. Fall was a very busy time for farmers—as well as planting grain crops, they had to pick the ripe grapes in September and harvest the olives (which were grown mainly for their oil) in late fall.

Left: The painting on this vase shows the olive harvest. One person is up in a tree picking olives, while two others shake the branches with sticks. Another gathers the fallen olives in a basket. Olive oil was used for cooking and burned in lamps.

Animals

The most common animals were sheep and goats, which were suited to the dry, stony land. They were kept for milk and wool, rather than to provide meat. Cows were also kept for their milk, and oxen were used for pulling plows. The Greeks also reared pigs and chickens.

Sheep and goats were grazed outside the villages on the dry hill-slopes, where they were watched over by shepherds. Milk from the animals was made into cheese, their wool was woven into cloth, and their skins were made into warm winter clothing.

Above: A cow with her calf.

Wine

Grapes were grown all over Greece. At harvest-time, a few bunches were kept for eating, and some were dried in the sun to make raisins.

But most of the grapes were used to make wine. They were tipped into huge pots, and people trampled on them to create a sticky mush. The resulting grape juice was then poured into jars and left until it turned into wine.

Crops

Barley was the most common crop. The grain was ground into flour for making bread and a kind of porridge. Some wheat was also grown (and some was imported), but wheat flour was more expensive. In the small fields surrounding each village, people grew fruit (apples, pears, and figs), vegetables (cabbages and onions), and legumes (chick peas and lentils).

Below: A clay figure of a farmer plowing his land. Plows—the most important farm tools—were strong wooden spikes with handles.

Daily chores for villagers included milking the goat, collecting eggs from the chickens, and checking that the cheeses and other goods were ready for market.

Below: A statue of the hero Herakles, posing as an archer and wearing elaborate plate armor. (His bow and arrow are now missing.) Poor soldiers, who could not afford spears, used bows and arrows, or slingshots for throwing stones.

Above: A dramatic scene from a siege, showing hoplites in front of a walled city, Lycia, fourth century B.C.

Weapons

The most deadly weapons were long spears, which could inflict very deep wounds. Soldiers also threw light spears at the enemy, shot them with arrows, and hurled stones using catapults. Weapons with sharp blades, such as swords, were also common. Catapults, flame-throwers, and battering rams were used for laying siege to cities.

War

War was common in ancient Greece and most men spent some time in the army. In Athens, all 18- to 20-year-old men trained as soldiers, while in Sparta, boys were taken away from their families at seven to train as soldiers. There was a major war between the Greeks and the Persians that lasted from 490 to 479 B.C., and Athens and Sparta fought a long and bitter war that lasted from 431 to 404 B.C.

❶ A GREEK TRIREME HAD THREE BANKS OF OARS.
❷ 170 OARSMEN ROWED THE SHIP INTO BATTLE, AIMING ITS RAM AT THE SIDE OF THE ENEMY SHIP. THEY HAD TO AVOID HITTING EACH OTHER'S OARS, ESPECIALLY AT TOP SPEED (ABOUT 10 MILES [16 KM] PER HOUR). OARSMEN WERE FROM THE LOWEST RANK OF SOCIETY, BUT WERE NOT SLAVES.
❸ THE MAIN DECK. ABOUT 10 OR MORE ARMED MEN WAITED ON DECK UNTIL THEY COULD BOARD THE ENEMY VESSEL.
❹ OAK RIBS PROVIDED THE FRAMEWORK OF THE SHIP.
❺ THE SAIL AND MAST WERE LOWERED IN BATTLE.

Left: This statuette is dedicated to Athena, the warrior goddess who was believed to be the protector of Athens.

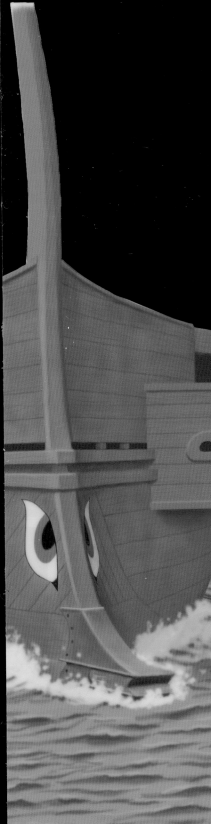

Soldiers

Greek armies were based on foot soldiers. Citizens who could afford to buy armor became hoplites, or armed men. They carried short, iron swords and long, iron-tipped spears. This equipment was extremely heavy, so on long marches slaves would carry it for their masters. The hoplites were the center of the army. Lighter-armed men were on either side; the poorest soldiers, with their rather more feeble arrows and stones, marched at the edges.

Left: A hoplite soldier wearing a bronze helmet, body armor, and greaves to protect his legs. He is carrying a bronze shield.

Greek hoplites fought in a tightly packed formation called a phalanx. The front ranks held out their spears while those behind them warded off the enemy's arrows.

Battles

On land, the two opposing armies would rush at each other and engage in close combat. A hoplite would aim his sword at an enemy soldier, who held up his own shield in defense. There would be deafening clashes of metal, or the slashing of flesh, or both. Soldiers often suffered horrific wounds to the neck and genitals, as these parts of the body were not protected by armor. Sea battles were fought by ramming the enemy ships at high speed, with the intention of damaging the ships so they would sink. The battle season lasted from March until October, when the men returned home to sow the crops.

Sparta

The army was central to Spartan society, and all Spartan men were required to join. At the age of seven, boys were taken away to live in army barracks, and there they stayed even after they were married.

Right: Detail from a bronze vase made by a Greek craft worker in Sparta in the late sixth century B.C. It shows fierce Spartan warriors and their war chariots. The foot soldiers wear elaborate helmets, and some carry large shields.

Warships

Many city-states, especially Athens, had large navies. The fastest ship of all was the trireme; 170 oarsmen were needed to row it. The prow had a pointed ram (right) for smashing into enemy ships.

Right: Statue of a Spartan warrior, fifth century B.C.

A bronze figure of Zeus, made in the mid-fifth century B.C. Zeus was the leader of the gods, and the god of justice. He was also lord of the sky—the rain god and cloud gatherer. When he was angry, he threw a terrible thunderbolt.

Religion

Religion was part of everyday life in ancient Greece. There were gods and goddesses for all areas of life and experience. Aphrodite, for example, was the goddess of love; Artemis, the goddess of hunting; and Ares, the rather unpopular god of war, who loved fighting. The Greeks liked to bargain with their gods. They believed that if they made promises and sacrifices, offered gifts, and held elaborate festivals in their honor, the gods would bring them health, happiness, and perhaps even wealth. Individual city-states had their own special gods—the goddess Hera, for example, was the protector of Samos. Religious festivals and feast days were held throughout the Greek calendar, and religious celebrations were also held to mark the major stages of a person's life.

Gods and goddesses

There were 12 main gods and many lesser ones. The most important lived on Mount Olympus and were members of Zeus's family. The shady gods of the Underworld were grouped around Hades, who ruled the kingdom of the dead without pity. The Greeks believed that their gods looked and behaved like humans—they could be selfish and cruel as well as good—but they never grew old or died.

Below: This beautiful terracotta statue of Demeter, the goddess of fertility and harvests, comes from Sicily. Every day, Greek families went to the altar in the courtyard of their houses and prayed to different gods, depending on the kind of help they needed. If they were about to harvest a crop, they prayed to Demeter.

Left: Part of this unusual drinking vessel is shaped like a goat's head. The rest is decorated with dancing maenads (frenzied women) and satyrs (part human, part animal). Both maenads and satyrs were worshipers of Dionysus, the god of fertility and wine. Mischievous satyrs were always dancing, playing tricks on people, and generally enjoying themselves. Dionysus was worshiped with great enthusiasm from the eighth century B.C. onward.

Above: A huge golden statue of Athena, the divine protector of Athens, stood in her temple, the Parthenon, for 900 years. The Greeks worshiped many goddesses, even though mortal women had no power in society.

Below: This procession of Greek citizens is making its way to a temple, where a bull is about to be sacrificed, and wine offered, to the gods. Slaves were not permitted to attend such festivals.

Left: A man consulting an oracle. An oracle was a place where a person went to seek the advice of the gods, especially if he had to make an important personal or political decision. A priest or priestess would interpret the god's answer and relay the message. But the replies were often vague, leading to great debates as to their meaning. In return for the advice, the person made a sacrifice or carried out a specific ritual. The most famous oracle was at Delphi, where the god Apollo could be questioned through a priestess.

Sacrifice and worship

It was common to sacrifice goats, sheep, horses, or oxen to the gods. The chosen animal was first groomed and adorned, and then led to the altar (it was important that it seemed willing to go). Then its head was pulled back to face the sky and its throat cut, at which point the women cried out. The animal was immediately skinned, chopped into pieces, and roasted. Participants ate the cooked meat—a rare treat for the poor. It was believed that the gods preferred the fat and bones, so the people ate the tasty meat!

Dancing maenads with their tambourines and thyrsus staffs. According to myth, maenads were female nature spirits. They could perform incredible feats, such as uprooting trees and tearing wild animals apart with their bare hands. Maenads were always present at Dionysus's wild parties.

Death and the afterlife

The Greeks had no strong belief in life after death. Most people thought that the spirits of the dead went to the Underworld, a grim place. A few good people might go to the Elysian Fields, a kind of paradise, or be turned into stars in the sky (like Castor and Pollux). A proper funeral, however, was important for the dignity of the dead.

A silver urn from the seventh century B.C. It was used to hold the ashes of a person who had been cremated.

The Olympic Games

Every four years, athletes from all over the Greek world gathered at Olympia for the Olympic Games. Warring armies would call a truce to allow competitors to attend. Events included running races, discus and javelin throwing, long jump, wrestling, and chariot racing. Athletes competed naked (and married women were forbidden to attend!).

In this modern ceremony, the Olympic torch is being lit from a burning flame at Olympia in Greece. The torch will be carried from Olympia by a team of runners to the country where the Games are to be held. The ceremony was inspired by the relay races of the ancient Olympics. These took place after dark using torches. The last runner of the winning team used his torch to light a fire at the altar to Zeus.

Festivals and Feast Days

A vase painting of a horse race. The vase was given as a prize at the Olympic Games.

The Greeks held many religious festivals throughout the year to please the gods. They were treated as public holidays, and were the only days off for working people (there were no weekends). On festival and feast days, wealthy women had the chance to get out of the house, and everyone had the opportunity to enjoy theatrical performances, as well as eating, drinking, dancing, and singing together. Sports festivals were extremely popular. As well as the famous Olympic Games, other games were held at Delphi, Nemea, and Corinth. The Greeks also held feasts at harvest-time and to celebrate weddings and birthdays.

The Panathenaic Festivals

The greatest festival in Athens in the fifth century B.C. was the Panathenea, held every four years to celebrate Athena's birthday. It was a spectacular affair involving singing, dancing, contests, and competitions. A huge procession of people carried cakes and other gifts to the Parthenon, where they were offered to the goddess, and a splendid robe was draped around her huge golden statue.

Left: This statue of a charioteer was found at Delphi, where chariot races were held in honor of the god Apollo. Winning the chariot race was such an achievement that the owner of the horses had a statue made to celebrate their victory. The charioteer is gripping one of the reins.

Above: This relief carving depicts three Athenian men carrying water jars up the hill to the Parthenon, as part of the magnificent Panathenaic procession. Hundreds of people gathered for the festival to celebrate Athena's birthday, and huge numbers of animals were sacrificed and eaten as part of the great feast.

Worshiping Dionysus

Two major festivals were held in honor of Dionysus, the god of fertility and wine. At the winter festival, women played the parts of maenads, allowing themselves to get into a frenzied state and praying that the earth would become fertile again. At the spring festival, up to 240 bulls were sacrificed for a feast and washed down with vast quantities of wine. The next day, favorite legends were acted out on stage, in front of a rowdy audience that cheered and booed loudly.

Left: A maenad dancing wildly with a snake in her hair and a live leopard in her hand. She decorated a fifth century B.C. drinking cup.

Right: A richly painted krater from the fourth century B.C., showing Dionysus and his followers making merry. A maenad is playing the double pipes. Other popular instruments played at festivals were harps, lyres, and pan pipes.

Left: A bride being taken to her new home after the wedding feast. The groom and his friends make up the procession. Only rich people had horse-drawn chariots; poor people had to walk. Newlyweds were showered with nuts and dried fruits—symbols of fertility.

Sports

Sporting contests formed part of the earliest religious festivals, and were held to honor the gods. At Olympia, the contests developed into the Olympic Games. The ancient Greeks believed that it was important for citizens to be strong and courageous so that they could fight well in times of war. Sporting contests allowed them to develop these qualities, and formed part of their military training. Activities included running races, long jump, javelin and discus throwing, wrestling, and ball games. The contests were dangerous, and competitors were often injured (sometimes even killed). Rules were strict, and those who broke them were severely punished. Winners gained great prestige and were thought of as heroes. Some people even believed that their statues could work miracles.

An oil vessel, used to hold oil for rubbing onto an athlete's body. The figure of the boy is perhaps tying on a ribbon that he has won in a sporting contest, or untying it to dedicate to one of the gods.

Right: These young men are playing an ancient version of hockey. The Greeks played various kinds of ball games, from rough-and-tough men's games to more gentle activities for the women at home.

Blood, sweat, and glory

The five-day Olympic Games (held every four years from 776 B.C.) gave the best opportunity for sportsmen to prove their skills. During the celebrations, outstanding athletes competed in the hot summer sun. Events such as running races required fitness and speed; other events tested the courage of the athletes as well. In the *pankration* contest—a mixture of wrestling and boxing— the only tactics that were banned were eye-gouging and biting. Winners received only a garland of wild olive leaves, but their fans rewarded them richly with gifts when they returned home.

Left: A group of young javelin-throwers in training. The painting decorated a lekythos, or oil flask, from the late sixth century B.C.

Right: This painting from a vase shows a chariot race, with spectators cheering on the competitors. The Olympic four-horse chariot race was dramatic and dangerous—many chariots crashed to the ground as they attempted the tight turns at each end of the race track.

Left: A decoration showing two women in a running race. Although it must have been hard to race in long dresses, all Greek women, except Spartans, had to remain covered up.

Women and sports

Unmarried women could compete in the female version of the Olympic Games, which was held to honor Zeus's wife, Hera. They raced on a track slightly shorter than the one used by men (five-sixths the length). Only in Sparta were women athletes allowed to train alongside men, and Spartan women were also allowed to wear short skirts for sports. Other Greeks thought that this was immoral and shocking.

Right: Wealthy men who did not have to work spent much of their time at the gymnasium (a kind of sports club). Before exercising, for example by wrestling, as shown here, the men undressed and washed and oiled their bodies. After their exercise, they scraped their skin clean with a curved metal instrument called a strigil, and took a relaxing bath in one of the rooms surrounding the open-air exercise area. When not exercising, the men often attended classroom discussions with philosophers. Over time, the gymnasia developed into the forerunners of modern universities.

The roar of the crowd

Sports contests were major public events. Men and unmarried women traveled from far and wide to attend the Olympic Games (only married women were not permitted to watch), and admission was free. Athletes played to the crowds to gain popularity. The expert wrestler Milo won the Olympic wrestling crown six times in the sixth century B.C. and was famous for his crowd-pleasing stunts. He would hold his breath until the pressure of the blood expanded his veins so much that they snapped a cord tied tight around his head!

This vase from Sparta is decorated with two wrestling scenes. In the larger scene, the man on the left has a bleeding nose, but the struggle continues. Spartans had a reputation throughout Greece for being incredibly tough.

The bearded wrestler on the right is about to hurl his opponent to the ground. To win, a wrestler had to throw the other man three times, pushing his shoulders to the ground each time.

Comedy and tragedy

The main types of drama were comedy and tragedy. Tragedies were written in verse, using solemn language, and often had plots involving fierce conflicts between humans and the gods. The problems were usually solved at the end of the plays, but only after much suffering and violence. Comedies were played for laughs. They were usually based on current issues and events, and poked fun at powerful or important people and the gods. Comedies were witty and often extremely rude, with lots of jokes about sex.

Actors wore masks representing different kinds of characters, but masks made it impossible to use facial expressions to give emphasis to their lines. All meaning depended on the actors' words and voices.

The players

There were usually only three actors on the stage at once. But most plays had many characters, so each actor had to play several different roles. The actors therefore wore different masks for each character. All actors were men, so they played all the female roles too. In addition, there was a chorus. This was made up of 15 people for tragedies, 24 for comedies, and 12 for the satyr plays. The chorus mostly performed songs and dances in the orchestra.

A terracotta statue of an actor playing a runaway slave, from the fourth century B.C. Masks such as the one he is wearing, and other props as well, were costly to produce. City officials used to choose a wealthy sponsor to help the theater by paying for such items.

A sculpted portrait of the Athenian writer of tragedies Sophocles (c. 496–406 B.C.). Sophocles' plays were very popular; he won the dramatic competition at least 20 times in 60 years. Along with the other famous tragic writers Aeschylus and Euripides, he often included women as active, central characters in his plays. This was a remarkable aspect of Greek tragedies, considering that they were written and performed by men.

❶ THE AREA WHERE THE AUDIENCE SAT WAS CALLED THE *THEATRON*. THE STONE SEATS WERE HARD AND UNCOMFORTABLE, AND PEOPLE OFTEN BROUGHT CUSHIONS WITH THEM.

❷ THE FIRST ROW OF SEATS WAS RESERVED FOR PEOPLE SUCH AS PRIESTS AND MAGISTRATES.

❸ THE *ORCHESTRA* WAS THE CIRCULAR AREA WHERE THE CHORUS PERFORMED. GREEK THEATERS WERE SO WELL DESIGNED THAT A COIN DROPPED IN THE CENTER OF THE *ORCHESTRA* COULD BE HEARD BY PEOPLE IN THE BACK ROW.

❹ ALL PARTS WERE PLAYED BY MALE ACTORS, WHO WORE MASKS.

❺ THE STAGE BUILDING WAS CALLED THE *SKENE*. SCENERY WAS PAINTED ONTO CANVAS AND HUNG ON THE *SKENE*.

❻ THE RAISED STAGE IN FRONT OF THE *SKENE* WAS THE *PROSKENION*.

Theater

Ancient Greeks loved the theater. The earliest performances took place at the festival of Dionysus. Competitions were held to see who could write the best play. By the fifth century B.C., there were three types of plays: tragedies, comedies, and plays with a chorus of satyrs. All proved extremely popular, and a passion for drama spread throughout the Greek world. Plays were performed in specially constructed theaters, with seating for up to 15,000 spectators. Performances could be rowdy affairs; members of the audience yelled their enthusiasm, complained loudly, or argued with their fellow spectators.

A fourth-century B.C. vase showing a scene from a comedy. The acrobat in the middle and the comic actor in the ugly mask to his right are looking toward the seated figure of Dionysus.

Popular entertainment

Going to the theater was a popular pastime. At the great spring festival of Dionysus in Athens, thousands of spectators would sit from dawn to dusk for several days in a row to watch the latest plays by the best playwrights. The whole population joined in the festival and everyday activities came to a standstill. Foreigners flocked to Athens to attend. Although few complete tragedies or comedies have survived, those that have are still performed today.

Left: Diagram of a hoist that was used to lift actors off the stage and make them "fly."

Below: Tunnels beneath the stage allowed actors to magically disappear.

Stage and set

Theaters had an orchestra—a semicircular floor in the middle of the theater—which was used by the chorus when there was action on the stage. Behind, the raised stage had a wall at the back with doors for the actors to enter. There was little scenery, though canvas scene paintings were used in later times.

Trade

The ancient Greeks had a long tradition of trading with other peoples. From the eighth century B.C., trading posts were established as far away as the Nile Delta in Egypt. Trade was busy between the city-states and the colonies, as well as with other Mediterranean countries. The main Greek exports were oil, wine, and luxury goods, including metalwork and pottery. The pottery was famous far and wide for its great beauty. Grain was imported to feed the growing population of mainland Greece, and the city-states also imported spices, salted fish, Egyptian papyrus, wood, wool, ivory, metals (such as gold, silver, and copper), and slaves. As the city-states grew wealthy, they built large merchant ships for carrying cargoes of goods all over the Mediterranean and farther afield.

Left: Official weights and measures of standard sizes were used for wet and dry goods—these official measures were found in the agora in Athens. Everyone had to use the same measures, and anyone who was caught selling a short measure was punished.

Coins were invented about the end of the seventh century B.C. in Lydia, Asia Minor (present-day Turkey), and their use for buying and selling gradually spread around the Greek world. The city-states issued their own coins as a sign of their independence. Usually made from gold or silver, coins often depicted a city's patron god or goddess. This silver coin (c. 490 B.C.) comes from the Macedon region.

Above: Hermes was the protector of travelers and merchants, and also shepherds. People prayed to him to give them a safe journey. In this Roman copy of a Greek bronze, he is shown at rest, wearing the winged sandals that symbolized his speedy movement.

Merchants

Small traders made goods to sell locally in the *agora*, or marketplace. Larger-scale merchants imported foreign goods and bought local produce to export. Business people often worked near a city's port. As the size of businesses grew, a banking system developed. Bankers lent money to merchants so that they could hire ships and buy cargo. When the merchants received payment for their goods, they paid back the loan. Interest rates on loans were high because shipping was such a dangerous business.

A gold comb with a finely decorated handle showing rival Scythians fighting around a dead horse. The Scythian warriors are equipped with imported Greek goods, such as the armor of the figure on the right and the helmet of the figure in the middle.

This perfume bottle in the shape of a horse's head was made on the Greek island of Rhodes—a major trading center. Luxury goods such as perfumes were imported from the East. Both perfumes and spices became far more common after Alexander the Great conquered part of India in the fourth century B.C. and founded the Greek-Indian kingdom of Bactria.

Trading partners

The colonies that the Greeks established overseas from the eighth century B.C. on gave them new trading partners. First they settled in southern Italy and Sicily; then in the seventh and sixth centuries B.C., they colonized the northern Aegean and Black Sea coasts, where traders sold luxury items in return for wheat. Colonies were also founded on the southern coasts of present-day Spain and France, in Cyrenaica (northeast Libya), Egypt, and Syria. Goods were bartered at first.

These amphorae—large, ceramic, two-handled pots—are from Mount Sinai (left) and Carthage (below); both date from the fifth to fourth centuries B.C. They were used to transport liquids such as olive oil or wine. Tens of thousands of amphorae, originally from Rhodes, were found in Egypt, proving that international trade was thriving in ancient times. The Rhodes' pots were all the same size and shape, and were made for exporting goods.

A pirate ship (right) in hot pursuit of a Greek merchant vessel, as shown on a cup painting from Athens. The word "pirate" comes from a Greek word meaning "sea-robber."

Dangers to shipping

Rough, stormy weather was always a worry for sailors on the high seas. If a ship was wrecked (as many were), the sailors stood little chance of survival. Many sunken wrecks laden with goods have been discovered in the Mediterranean. Piracy was another major problem. Powerful city-states such as Athens sometimes sent out a fleet of warships to protect a convoy of merchant ships.

This merchant ship is loading a valuable cargo, stored in amphorae, for transportation along one of the major trade routes.

Transport

There were few good roads in mountainous ancient Greece. Most Greeks lived near the sea, and the easiest way to carry goods was by ship. Huge merchant ships, powered by sails and oars, were used to transport goods over long distances. For short journeys overland, people relied on donkeys to carry their heavy loads up and down steep mountain tracks. Horses, mules, donkeys, or oxen pulled wheeled carts.

The *Agora*

A man having his hair cut by a barber. The barber's shop was a favorite meeting place for men and offered an excellent opportunity to catch up on the latest news.

The *agora* was the lively hub of every Greek town and city. An open space either in the center of the city or near the harbor, it was the place to shop, meet friends, and find out what was going on in the world. At its heart was a bustling market, with stalls selling everything from vegetables to sheepskins and slaves. There were workshops where craftworkers labored in iron and bronze, or made pots, shoes, bags, jewelry, weapons, or musical instruments. Wealthy women were forbidden to go to the *agora*, so men did the shopping. Poorer women shopped there and sold their wares. The *agora* was surrounded by temples and important public buildings, such as the council chamber and law courts.

A typical scene in the agora *in Athens. The* agora *was packed with many small traders selling fish, fruit, and vegetables, and providing services. People could get their shoes mended there, have their hair cut, and buy slaves, furniture, pottery, animals, or gifts.*

Town planning

By the fifth century B.C., the Greeks were building new towns and rebuilding old ones to a proper plan. New towns were designed with a neat grid of streets that divided the town into blocks. Different zones of the town were used for different purposes—there were residential areas of private housing, and zones for public use. The way in which towns grew up depended on the type of government, too. When tyrants were in power, they were more interested in spending money on large, impressive buildings such as temples. After the birth of democracy in Athens, public buildings such as the council chamber and *stoa* were built around the *agora*. The *stoa* was a narrow building with an open colonnade along one side that provided protection from the sun and rain. Men would gather there to meet their friends and chat about local events.

Politics, power, and gossip

When new laws were passed or there was a military call-up, the *agora* was the place to hear the news. Most decisions were made by the rich and powerful in the public buildings surrounding the *agora*, such as the council house, the law courts, and the court of appeal. The public notice-board gave all the details. Those who could read passed on the information to others. In this way, the *agora* fulfilled the role of the media in the Greek world.

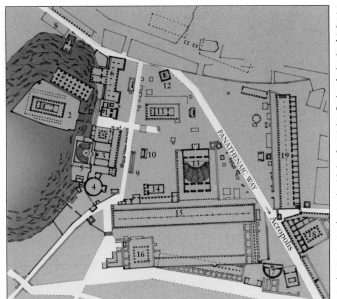

1 *Temple of Apollo Patroos*
2 *Temple of Hephaestus*
3 *Metroon*
4 *Tholos*
5 *New Bouleterion*
6 *Stoa of Zeus Eleutherios*
7 *Hellenistic building*
8 *Sanctuary of Demos and Graces*
9 *Eponymous Heroes*
10 *Altar of Zeus Agoraios*
11 *Temple of Ares*
12 *Altar of 12 Gods*
13 *Odeion of Agrippa*
14 *Roman temple*
15 *Middle stoa*
16 *Heliaia*
17 *Nymphaeum*
18 *Library of Pantainos*
19 *Stoa of Attalos*

A plan of the agora *in Athens in the second century* A.D. *The many functions of the* agora *are evident from its buildings. There were temples and altars, stoas, a library, and the public notice-board. The tholos* was a circular building where up to 50 council officials had dinner—paid for by the government—and made sacrifices.

A vase painting showing a man cutting a large fish steak for a customer.

Shopping

Wealthy women were not allowed to go out, except to attend religious ceremonies and family celebrations. So men or slaves did the shopping at the markets (which were not always in the *agora*). Food had to be bought fresh every day. In the *agora*, stalls selling the same kinds of produce, such as olive oil, cheese, or wine, were probably grouped in certain areas. Officials called *metronomoi* made sure that traders used the correct weights and measures, and did not cheat their customers. Overseers (*agoranomoi*) kept order and checked the quality of the goods on sale.

This vase-painting depicts a blacksmith's workshop. The man on the left is using tongs to hold a piece of hot metal, and another man is about to beat it into shape with an ax. The men may be slaves; they are being supervised by the man on the far right, who is probably their owner. A variety of tools hangs on the wall behind them.

An Athenian silver coin. Each city-state had its own currency, so visitors had to exchange their cash at a money-changer's stall in the agora.

Art

This bowl is decorated with eyes, such as those painted on the prows of ships. It features Castor and Pollux, the gods of shipwrecked sailors.

Over a period of more than 1,000 years, the ancient Greeks created an enormous variety of sculpture, painting, pottery, poetry, and music—the inspiration for much of Western art in later times. There was a huge development of artistic styles, from the Archaic period (660–480 B.C.), through the Classical period (480–330 B.C.), to the Hellenistic period (330–30 B.C.). Sculpture started with rather stiff-looking figures made to honor the gods, but developed into graceful, lifelike figures of people doing everyday things. From the mid-seventh to fifth century B.C., statues were used to mark graves. Later, they were built to stand in sanctuaries or public places. Pottery was styled with intricate patterns using techniques such as black- or red-figure painting. Poets wrote epics of adventure, which were recited and accompanied by music.

An Athenian vase (c. 690 B.C.) decorated with sphinxes (monsters with human heads and the bodies of lions), a piper and dancers, and chariots.

This bronze sculpture shows the hero Odysseus hiding underneath a ram. Homer's Odyssey tells how he did this to escape the fearsome Cyclops—a one-eyed giant.

Epic poetry

Greek poetry was usually sung or chanted. Epic poems were extremely long and related the heroic deeds of gods and men. They were usually loosely based on events from the past. The oldest-surviving epic poems are the *Iliad* and *Odyssey*, which were told by Homer—the first great poet of European literature.

This eighth-century B.C. figure from Crete is of a bard—a person who recited poems—playing a lyre. The main purpose of music was to accompany poetry and dance.

Many Greek potters used a wheel to help mold clay into vessels. As the wheel turned, they shaped the clay into beautiful vases. Some pots, especially large storage jars, were made without a wheel, just by hand.

Vase painting

The earliest vases, from the 10th and 9th centuries B.C. (the Geometric period), were decorated with abstract patterns of circles, triangles, zigzags, and lines. In the next phase, the Archaic period (660–480 B.C.), human and animal figures became popular. From the early sixth century B.C., Athenian artists used the "black-figure" technique to decorate their pots with black designs on cream or red backgrounds. Details were either incised or painted on. Then, about 530 B.C., "red-figure" painting became fashionable. Outlines were drawn into red clay, and details were painted with brown lines. The rest of the pot was painted with a black glaze.

This pelike is decorated in the "red-figure" style and shows a battle between gods and giants. Scenes from mythology were popular until about the 450s B.C.

The human body in sculpture

Sculptures from the Archaic period (660–480 B.C.) are not particularly realistic—they look rigid and often have tight-lipped smiles—but they show the beginnings of a desire by Greek artists to depict the human form. In Classical sculpture (from 480 B.C.), the human form was much more lifelike, and artists showed a greater understanding of how the human body really looks and moves. In 451 B.C., an artist named Polyclitus of Argos created sculptures of athletes that almost seemed to move. Toward the end of the Classical period, sculptors mastered a greater range of expressions and were able to show human emotions more realistically than ever before.

Left: A bronze statue of a warrior, found in Riace, southern Italy, from the fifth century B.C. The Greeks loved naked male figures—athletes and gods were especially popular subjects. Nude female statues did not appear until the next century.

Statue of a Greek woman (530 B.C.), from the Acropolis in Athens. Life-size statues of people were sculpted from marble during the seventh and sixth centuries B.C. Those of women (clothed) were known as "korai," and those of men (naked) were called "kouroi."

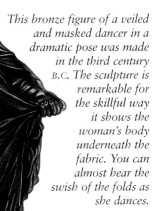

This bronze figure of a veiled and masked dancer in a dramatic pose was made in the third century B.C. The sculpture is remarkable for the skillful way it shows the woman's body underneath the fabric. You can almost hear the swish of the folds as she dances.

Bronzes

To make a bronze statue, artists often used the "lost wax" method. They made a rough shape from clay and sculpted a wax model around it. After covering the wax over with more clay, they fired it, which melted the wax. Molten bronze was poured into the cavity left by the melted wax. Bronze statues were often decorated with red copper for lips and nipples, silver for teeth, and glass or stones for the eyes.

Above: A red-figure vase painting of a sculptor's workshop (fourth century B.C.).

An artist decorating a pot. Pots for special occasions were expertly painted and then left to dry, before being fired in a kiln.

This marvelous bronze head, skillfully carved in great detail about 460–440 B.C., is regarded by some as the earliest example of a true Greek portrait.

Portraits

Portrait statues started to become popular in the fourth century B.C. The early portraits were of dead people, and they idealized the subjects, rather than showing exact likenesses. But in Hellenistic times (323–146 B.C.), portraits of living people were made, too, and these were more realistic. As well as depicting elite rulers, generals, and philosophers, artists began to sculpt ordinary people—including the aged, and women and children—in natural poses.

Columns

The Greeks developed three styles of architecture—Doric, Ionic, and Corinthian. Each had its own type of column for supporting the upper section of the temple. The main styles were Doric and Ionic. A: The older Doric columns were strong and simple, with a plain capital (top). B: Ionic columns were slender and ornamental; the capitals were decorated with scrolls. C: Corinthian columns were more decorative. The capital is covered with acanthus-leaf designs. Columns were constructed in drum-shaped sections, which were pegged together to keep them from wobbling or falling down.

A

B

C

Above: This is the porch of the Erectheum, a temple on the Acropolis in Athens, where some of the finest buildings in the Greek world are to be found. Instead of standard columns, the figures of lovely young women in beautifully draped robes hold up the roof. They are called "caryatids." The three temples and the entrance to the Acropolis were completed in just over 40 years—incredibly fast for ancient times.

Architecture

The Greeks lived in quite simple homes, but built splendid temples and public buildings. Temples were the homes of their gods and therefore deserved their very best efforts. Early temples were often made from mud-brick, but later magnificent stone temples were built all over Greece and the Greek colonies. Except in Crete, people were not able to go into the temples to see their gods and worship there. Religious ceremonies were performed at altars outside. From the fifth century B.C., Greek architects also turned their attention to creating beautiful public buildings such as *stoas* and council buildings.

❶ 20,000 TONS (18,200 T) OF STONE BLOCKS WERE USED TO BUILD THE PARTHENON.

❷ THE PARTHENON WAS SURROUNDED BY 46 MARBLE DORIC COLUMNS. EACH COLUMN WAS MADE OF DRUM-SHAPED SECTIONS THAT WERE PEGGED TOGETHER TO KEEP THEM FROM WOBBLING OR FALLING DOWN.

❸ A 32-FOOT-HIGH (10 M) STATUE OF ATHENA, THE PROTECTOR OF ATHENS, STOOD INSIDE. IT WAS MADE OF GOLD AND IVORY BY THE SCULPTOR PHIDIAS, AND WAS DRESSED IN ARMOR.

The Parthenon, the largest building on the Acropolis in Athens, was constructed in the fifth century B.C. Inside was a 33-foot-tall (10 m) gold and ivory statue of Athena, the divine protector of Athens.

In 490 B.C., the Athenians won a victory in their war against the Persians at the Battle of Marathon. Three years later, they built a Doric marble treasury (right) as a symbol of their triumph and strength. It was filled with the treasures that they had captured from the Persians. The building was also a temple to Apollo, the god of art, archery, and male beauty.

Civic buildings

The Greeks created special buildings for the men who participated in government. The Council met in the *bouleterion* (Council house), which had a large room with tiers of seats on three sides. The *prytaneis*, the top council committee, entertained ambassadors in the *pryteneion*; some Hellenistic *prytaneia* were like private houses with an inner courtyard. Members of the *prytaneis* met in a circular *tholos*, which looked like a temple. Other public buildings included the *stoa* (a long, narrow, sheltered building where citizens gathered), temples, and theaters.

④ ATHENA IS HOLDING A STATUE OF THE WINGED FIGURE NIKE (VICTORY).

⑤ THE NAVE OF THE TEMPLE WAS CALLED THE CELLA. BEHIND IT WAS A SMALLER CHAMBER, WHERE SACRED VESSELS AND PRIESTS' ROBES WERE KEPT.

⑥ ON THE EASTERN PEDIMENT, A SCULPTED FRIEZE DEPICTED THE BIRTH OF ATHENA.

In Magna Grecia, the Greek colonies along the southern coast of Italy, the ecclesiasterion was constructed as a meeting place for the ecclesia— the assembly of all the citizens. Even where there were tyrants in power, citizens were allowed to have their say in government. This ecclesiasterion (left), dating from the fifth century B.C., is from Paestrum in Italy.

Health and Medicine

The early Greeks trusted magic and rituals to bring them good health and cure their illnesses. They believed that disease was a punishment from the gods, so they prayed to Asclepius, the god of medicine, to cure them. Sick people spent the night in the sanctuary to Asclepius, where the god appeared to them and recommended a treatment. A priest carried out the treatment, which was often an herbal remedy. Some people were cured, but if the patient looked as if he was likely to die, the priest would refuse to treat him. From the fifth century B.C., Greek doctors developed scientific treatments that were not bettered for hundreds of years. Hippocrates was the most famous Greek doctor. He understood the importance of preventing disease in the first place and gave people sensible advice about diet and exercise.

Left: A statue of Asclepius, the god of medicine, from Roman times. His sacred snake is twisted around his staff. The snake was said to have given him an herb that healed all diseases and even brought the dead back to life.

This Greek doctor is giving an herbal remedy to a child to cure his illness. He has made the medicine from a selection of dried plants. Leaves or roots were often crushed in a mortar with a pestle to extract their oil. The doctor has recorded his herbal remedies on parchment scrolls.

Prognosis, plants, and prescriptions

The Greeks thought that illness came from an imbalance between the four humors of the body: blood, phlegm, yellow bile, and black bile. But they were less interested in discovering the cause of a disease than in predicting the outcome—the prognosis. A doctor's reputation rested on his ability to predict who would recover and who would die. Doctors used many herbal remedies. Theophrastus (third century B.C.) recommended a treatment for wounds that contained cinnamon—and it is now proven that oil of cinnamon kills germs.

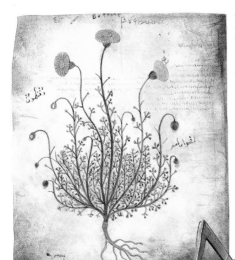

An illustration of a plant from a medical book of the first century A.D. Different parts of plants—the roots, leaves, or flowers— were used to make cures. Cannabis was prescribed to relieve earache.

These surgical instruments from Hellenistic times include knives, scalpels, tweezers, and a medicine box.

A bust of Hippocrates. The Hippocratic Oath, named for him (although he didn't write it), is still sworn by doctors today. They swear to work for the benefit of the patient and never to be involved in "mischief and corruption."

Hippocrates

The famous physician Hippocrates (c. 460–c. 377 B.C.) is sometimes called the "father of medicine." He taught that the body was a whole, and that each part could be understood only in the context of the whole. He also rejected the popular belief that diseases were a punishment from the gods, and instead declared that they had natural causes. He saw that fat people were likely to die younger than slim people, and asserted that a healthy lifestyle, exercise, and a good diet were essential. Hippocrates's experiments included taking body substances, such as ear wax or vomit, and testing them by tasting them!

Surgery

Surgery in ancient Greece was extremely painful by today's standards, but was sophisticated for the times. Hippocrates and his followers wrote 70 books about all aspects of medicine, including various kinds of surgery, and they were clearly very skilled. In their writings, they explain how to set up an operating theater, carry out various operations on fractured and dislocated bones, and dress wounds afterward. The Greeks also did some dental work, such as pulling out teeth, but they did not use fillings.

Head of the goddess Hygeia, the daughter of Asclepius, the god of medicine. The image of a healthy person, she was always shown looking beautiful. Hygeia did not heal disease, but looked after a person's good health through common sense behavior, such as keeping clean. The word "hygiene" derives from her name.

Doctors

Greek doctors were famous for their skills. Some earned top salaries treating their rulers, or working as city doctors paid by the government. Others did not have such high status. Doctors tended to move from town to town, setting up a surgery (*iatreion*) to work from. In addition to Hippocrates, other famous Greek doctors included Herophilus (335–280 B.C.), who was the first to cut up dead bodies to investigate what lay inside. A later doctor, Galen (A.D. 130–200), was not allowed to cut up human bodies, but he is known to have dissected monkeys, pigs, dogs, and even an elephant.

A stone relief of a doctor or priest working on a patient. A nurse or priestess is helping him. Doctors learned their skills by being apprenticed to an experienced physician as an assistant or nurse.

Education and Learning

Plato opened a philosophy school in Athens. He followed Socrates' teaching methods and wrote down many of his master's ideas. Plato thought it was vital for young, ambitious men to study philosophy, so they would be good and fair when in power.

In most Greek towns, boys went to school from age seven. All schools were private (the city-states did not build them), and only families who could afford the fees sent their boys to school. But the fees were not very expensive, as teaching was neither highly respected nor well paid. At school, boys learned reading, writing, and math, as well as singing, dancing, and poetry. They spent a lot of time boxing, wrestling, and running to toughen themselves up for the army. Girls were mostly educated at home. They learned how to keep house and prepare for married life. If they were lucky, they were taught to read and write, and perhaps to play musical instruments.

Philosophy

Philosophy means the "love of knowledge." It involves trying to find out about things by reasoning. In ancient Greece, it covered a wide range of subjects, including science, society, morality, and religion. Philosophers argued that events were the result of natural causes, not the work of the gods. But they came up with some strange ideas, too. The followers of Pythagoras, for example, would not eat beans because they believed they contained the souls of the dead.

Socrates (470–399 B.C.) was a great philosopher. He tried to find out the truth about things by asking searching questions, such as "What is a good man?" But the leaders of Athenian society distrusted him because he encouraged young men to question their belief in the gods. He was put on trial and executed.

A boy being taught by his teacher. Boys were accompanied to school by a slave called a paidogogus. The slave was allowed to beat the boy if he did not behave properly.

A bust of Aristotle, one of the most famous Greek philosophers. He wrote about many aspects of human knowledge.

Schools

Schools in Sparta and Athens developed differently. In Sparta, they provided military training for boys ages 7 to 20. The boys were housed in barracks and were taught physical endurance and agility through sports and dancing, and only basic reading and writing skills. In Athens, some boys went to day schools, and they could continue their education up to age 18 with private tutors if their parents could afford to pay. In Hellenistic times, schools called *gymnasia* were set up for older boys and girls. They learned philosophy, literature, music, math, and science, and did physical training.

A reading lesson, shown on the inside of an Athenian cup from 430 B.C. The man (seated) is reading from a scroll and the boy is reading from a folded wooden tablet.

A well-rounded education

There were three main areas of education in fifth-century B.C. Athens: literature, physical education, and music. Once they could read and write, boys had to learn grammar. They were expected to memorize parts of lengthy epic poems, especially Homer's *Iliad* and *Odyssey*, and to discuss questions raised by the author. Special teachers taught sport, and it was important to shine as a sportsman. Students also learned to play a musical instrument and to dance.

A schoolboy practices his lyre in front of his sister. The soundbox of the lyre was made from a turtleshell.

Literacy

Most ancient Greeks were illiterate. Some poor people learned to read and write a little through their trade, but few could do more than sign their names. Wealthy boys who learned to read and write at school practiced their handwriting on wooden tablets covered in wax, writing with a bone or metal stylus. By the fifth century B.C., most Athenian citizens were probably literate.

A statue of Athena, the goddess of wisdom, wearing a gown of live snakes (probably from the sixth century B.C.). She was often portrayed with an owl—the symbol of wisdom—sitting on her shoulder.

Math and geometry

The Greeks had great success in math. The followers of Pythagoras tried to explain the order of the universe using patterns of numbers. They then turned to geometry. Euclid, who taught at Alexandria in Egypt about 300 B.C., developed geometrical principles (to do with the relationships of lines, angles, and shapes) that are still used today. Archimedes (287–212 B.C.) worked out the approximate value of *pi*, used for measuring circles, and thought of a way of working with very large numbers. The Greeks also made advances in astronomy and physics.

A bust of the philosopher and mathematician Pythagoras (c. 580–500 B.C.). Pythagoras developed the view that the world was based on mathematical patterns.

A mosaic of Anaximander, a philosopher. In about 550 B.C., he drew the first world map showing Earth from above as a rounded shape. He also invented a sundial to measure time.

Knowledge and influence

Greek thinkers were influenced by both the Egyptians (the inventors of geometry) and the Babylonians, who—like the Egyptians—knew some astronomy. Ancient Greek knowledge, in turn, had a great impact on later societies. People in Europe learned about ancient Greek ideas in medieval times, from Arab scholars. Much of Greek knowledge, such as dissection, was not improved on for many centuries. Our own language and alphabet have roots in ancient Greek, and the ideas of the philosophers are still discussed today.

These clay spoons have been hand-painted and the handles shaped into animal heads.

Food and Cooking

The ancient Greeks had a simple, healthy diet based on cereals, vegetables, cheese, legumes, fish, and olive oil. Herbs and spices were used to flavor dishes—people liked strong, sour, and bitter tastes. Most people survived on bread and vegetables, but the wealthy enjoyed more exotic dishes at dinner parties. Grasshoppers and cicadas were favorite appetizers, for example. Women were regarded as better cooks than men, so cooking was their job. They usually cooked outdoors in the central courtyard of their house, sitting on the ground around a stove or brazier.

Wine

Wine was the most common drink in ancient Greece. It was so thick that it needed to be strained and then diluted with water. Sometimes it was spiced and flavored, or even heated to make a warming winter drink. Even at breakfast, people ate bread dipped in wine and water. Poor people drank the lowest quality wine, or drank water or goats' milk. There was no tea or coffee in ancient Greece.

Below: A terracotta statue of a woman grinding grain into flour using a hand-mill. It dates from fifth-century B.C. Athens.

This large "red-figure" storage vase from about 450 B.C. shows a woman using a ladle to serve wine.

The inside of this cup is decorated with a huntsman and his dog. He has caught a fox and a hare. Meat was generally eaten only at festivals, although wealthy people were able to hunt wild deer, boar, and hares.

Below: A figure of a woman shaping dough into loaves. Bread was baked in fired clay ovens that were heated with smoldering charcoal. As well as ordinary bread and flat bread, the Greeks made cookies, cakes, and pastries sweetened with honey.

Bread and cereals

Bread was a staple in the Greek diet. It was usually made from barley. The poorest women had to grind the grain into flour and make bread every day; wealthier people had slaves to do this for them. Large cities had bakeries where people could buy their loaves. Barley was also made into a thick porridge that was eaten with vegetables for the evening meal. Other cereals included rye and spelt, which grew well in the harsh, dry climate. Wheat was imported, which made it expensive. Only rich people could afford wheat bread.

Olives

Olives were the third most important crop after cereals and grapes. The Greeks ate olives as a side dish and cooked all kinds of food in olive oil. In fact, olives were so important to the Greeks that, in times of war, one side would often cut down their enemy's olive trees to deprive them of the valuable olive oil.

Fish and seafood

Most towns and villages were close to the sea and had a daily fish market, where fish and shellfish were sold. Fish was a very popular food, and was eaten fresh, dried, or pickled. There are stories of "fish gluttons," who gorged themselves on fish; one writer describes someone who nearly died eating a three-foot-long (1 m) octopus!

A plate decorated with fish and used to serve fish dishes. Thick sauce was poured into the well in the middle of the plate. Diners dipped morsels of fish into the sauce and ate the tender mouthfuls.

Dinner parties

Greek men loved to go to *symposia* (dinner parties) at friends' houses. They gathered to eat, drink, sing, dance, and be entertained by beautiful young girls and boys. The party took place in the tastefully decorated *andron*—a room used only by male guests. The men reclined on couches, propped up on their left elbows. They were served tasty delicacies, which they ate with their fingers, and drank fine wine. Sometimes a great philosopher was invited to the *symposion* to discuss his theories, giving the event a more serious atmosphere.

These men are enjoying a feast of cheese, wine, olives, and probably a number of bird dishes. A great variety of birds were eaten at feasts, including ducks, geese, thrushes, and nightingales. The food is served to the guests by slaves.

A slave carrying a table. Tables were usually made of wood. They were easy to move; a table of food was brought to the guest rather than the other way around.

Furniture

The Greeks liked simple, light furniture that had different purposes and could be moved around. Couches were used for sleeping as well as dining; sometimes diners simply fell asleep where they were! Tables were low and had three legs, which helped to balance them on uneven earth floors. Chairs had stiff backs and arms, with cushions or animal skins to make them comfortable. Four-legged stools were used all over the home. The Greeks did not place ornaments or valuables on tables—they were for food and food alone.

❶ THE WALLS OF GREEK HOUSES WERE MADE OF FLIMSY MUD-BRICK. BURGLARS WERE KNOWN TO BREAK IN THROUGH THE WALLS!

❷ WOMEN HAD THEIR OWN QUARTERS (THE *GYNAIKONITIS*) ON THE UPPER FLOOR, WHERE THEY SPUN WOOL AND WOVE IT INTO CLOTH ON A LOOM.

❸ MEN ENTERTAINED VISITORS IN THE MORE PUBLIC *ANDRON*, OFTEN THE MOST DECORATED ROOM IN THE HOUSE.

❹ WINE AND PRECIOUS GRAIN WERE KEPT IN STORE ROOMS.

A fifth-century B.C. terracotta relief showing a woman placing carefully folded linen in an elaborately decorated chest. Chests were used for storing clothes, blankets, and other household goods.

Women airing clothes, using a contraption hanging from the ceiling. The Greeks didn't like to have clutter around the room, so they used the walls—and in this case, the ceiling—for hanging things. Pots, pans, and tools of all kinds were hung on the walls.

⑤ IN THE KITCHEN, COOKING WAS DONE IN A STONE OVEN OR OVER A BRAZIER. POTS WERE HUNG ON THE WALLS.

⑥ THE BATHROOM HAD A BATHTUB AND, SOMETIMES, A LARGE POT, USED FOR A TOILET.

⑦ BEDS WERE SIMPLE, AND CLOTHES WERE KEPT FOLDED IN CHESTS.

⑧ THE COURTYARD HAD AN ALTAR, AND ALSO A WELL FOR DRAWING WATER.

Women

Women were responsible for running the household, keeping the family's accounts, caring for the children, and making clothes. In wealthy households, most of the work was done by slaves, with the mistress supervising. Women spent their time in the *gynaikonitis*, a separate part of the house out of bounds for men.

The figures of two women, in painted terracotta, from Classical times. Women spent most of their time with children and with other female members of the family. Relationships between women must have been close.

At Home

Greek homes were not usually elaborate, since most people—except wealthy women—spent most of their lives outdoors. Houses were built of mud-brick walls with a flattened earth floor. The courtyard was the heart of the home, where food was cooked and children and pets ran about. The family altar was in the center. Around the courtyard were the rooms, with separate areas for men and women. For water, people might have a well; otherwise, they had to walk to the fountain house. There were no toilets, so people used a back alley or communal toilet outdoors. Rich people had bigger homes but enjoyed only slightly more comfort.

This fifth-century B.C. oil lamp was used to provide light at nighttime. The lamp contained a bowl for the olive oil, a nozzle for the wick, and handles.

A small bronze figure of a baby learning to crawl. Babies must have been much happier once their swaddling was removed, and they were able to move.

Babies

Babies were born at home, with all the women of the household present. A midwife sometimes helped, and a doctor was called if there were problems. In Athens (but not in Sparta), small babies were swaddled, or wrapped in bandages, to keep them from moving. Mothers usually breastfed their babies.

A lekythos, or oil flask, showing a servant girl carrying a child, and the mother attending.

Children

Childhood was a struggle for survival in ancient Greece. Many babies died soon after birth, and some were rejected and left abandoned if they looked like they were too weak to survive. Children were brought up by their mothers. In wealthy families, both girls and boys spent their early years at home, where they had a huge variety of toys to play with (many similar to modern ones). Then, at age seven, Athenian boys started school, and Spartan boys and girls went to live in the military school. The children of poor families worked with their parents in the fields, in workshops, or in the *agora*.

Childcare

Greek women liked to bring up their children themselves, rather than letting servants do it all for them. Mothers fed, washed, and changed their own babies. Wealthy Greeks had plenty of help from a nurse, a *paidagogus* (a slave who accompanied a boy to school), and household slaves. Women often spent more time with their children than with their husbands, and perhaps felt closer to them.

Growing up the Greek way

Babies who survived childbirth were checked over by the father. If he thought the baby did not look healthy, it was left in a public place to die or be rescued by someone else and, usually, brought up as a slave. Babies who were accepted by the father were welcomed into the family with a naming ceremony when they were 10 days old. At age 12 or 13, children were considered young adults. They had to stop playing with their toys and deliver them to the temple. At about age 15, girls were married to older men.

Girls were seen as less important than boys, and were more frequently abandoned as newborn babies. The girls that a father decided to keep were taught at home. Their mother instructed them in all the household tasks of cooking, spinning, weaving, and childcare. Wealthy girls rarely left the house except to go to religious festivals. Poor girls learned a trade or accompanied their mothers to sell goods in the agora.

Dogs were the most common kind of pet, but children loved to play with cats and other small animals, too.

Pets

Children played in the family courtyard with a variety of pets. Dogs were kept as companions as well as working animals, and pigs, tortoises, and caged birds were common, too. Children also kept insects such as grasshoppers, and wealthy children sometimes had cranes or geese. Some pets, such as roosters, were set to fight each other—a cruel but popular pastime.

Young men boxing, shown on a fresco at the palace at Knossos, Crete, around 1700–1400 B.C. Physical fitness was considered extremely important, especially for boys, and they practiced wrestling and boxing from a young age.

Toys for all

The ancient Greeks made many toys at home and bought others from the *agora*. A baby's first toy was probably a rattle with pebbles inside. Older children played on swings, seesaws, and hobbyhorses—and it is said that the Greeks invented the kite. Children also played with hoops, model carts, and chariots. For imaginative play, they had animal figures, toy furniture, and clay or rag dolls.

Children who died young were often buried with their favorite toys. These terracotta models of a doll on a chair and some boots were found in a girl's tomb from c. 420 B.C.

Left: Terracotta figures were popular toys. This goose with a rider is unusual; generally such figures were of a horse and rider.

Games

Greek children played leapfrog and gave each other piggyback rides. They also played a game in which one child wearing a blindfold had to try to catch his or her friends. A team game like hockey was played with a ball made from a pig's bladder. For quiet play, children enjoyed dice and board games, and a game called knucklebones, which was popular with girls—the players flicked small animal bones into the gaps between their fingers.

This detail from a vase decoration shows a procession of children, with a maypole and cart, on its way to the festival of Dionysus. Religious events such as the Dionysus festival gave girls from wealthy families a rare opportunity to leave the house.

A Hellenistic statue of a young athlete in a short cloak. He is shown at rest, leaning against a turning-post beside a running track.

Clothing and Makeup

Both men and women wore long, loose garments, ideal for the warm summers. In winter, they added a thick, woolen cloak over the top. Brightly colored clothes were popular, especially among women, but poor people could probably afford only plain, undyed material. In the countryside, laborers wore leather cloaks, or jerkins (sleeveless jackets) made from animal skins. Footwear ranged from sandals and shoes to boots. Women liked to wear elaborate hairstyles, and cosmetics were popular. Underwear was not always worn (by men or women)—and it was bad manners to lift up a tunic in public!

Above: In the seventh and sixth centuries B.C., Greek women wore their long hair loose, fastened by a headband or headdress, as in this statue. From the fifth century B.C., women started to pile up their hair into an elegant knot, which they held in place with a net and ribbons. Slave women wore their hair cut short.

People usually wore lengths of woolen cloth draped about the body in different ways. The garment worn by the man on the right indicates that he is a citizen, while the other man's robe shows he is a workman. Workmen wore a himation, *a rectangle of cloth worn gathered over one shoulder, with the other arm bare.*

Right: The wealthy woman on this vase is wearing an elegant garment of contrasting colors. Cloth was dyed using plant dyes (such as from nettles and lichens) or animal dyes (from insects and snails). Saffron yellow was a favorite color with women.

Makeup

Women, and sometimes men, wore perfumes and cosmetics. It was fashionable to have a pale face, so women painted their faces with white lead (not knowing it was poisonous). They used rouge to give their cheeks color, and put soot or charcoal on their eyebrows and eyelids to emphasize them. Greek women liked red or green eyeshadow, and they painted their lips, too.

Left: Statue of a woman wearing a peplos. *The cloth of a peplos was longer than the wearer, and more than twice as wide. It was held at the shoulders with pins or long spikes—one pair found was 18 inches (46 cm) long!*

Clothes for all seasons

A basic item of clothing was the *chiton*, a tunic generally worn over a *himation* by men, or over a *peplos* by women. The *peplos*, the standard item of dress for women, was itself something between a cloak and a tunic. It was a rectangle of cloth with the top section folded over and secured with pins at the shoulders, leaving both arms bare. It became less fashionable in the cities by about 300 B.C., though country women continued to wear it, especially when the weather was cold.

A scene painted on an epinetron *(a knee-guard used while working on wool) showing a bride (far right) and her friends in the women's quarters, c. 430 B.C. The women are helping the bride choose jewelry for her wedding.*

Footwear

Footwear ranged from the simplest toe-strap sandals to lace-up or pull-on boots, and tough hobnail boots for soldiers. Warm wool or sheepskin boots kept people's feet warm in winter. Shoes were usually made of leather, but wood was also used. Short women liked to wear thick-soled shoes to make them taller. The Greeks needed strong, sensible shoes for all the walking they did. But they often went barefoot outdoors, and they always took their shoes off when they went into the house.

In this shoemaker's workshop, the man sitting on the floor is cutting leather to make the soles of some shoes. Another shoemaker is drawing the outline of his customer's feet onto a piece of leather so that he can craft a pair of shoes to the right size and shape.

Above: A bronze mirror used when applying makeup.

Right: A fourth-century B.C. gold earring in the shape of a boat.

Below: An eighth-century B.C. earring with delicate gold decoration, and right, a ninth-century B.C. gold earring.

Jewelry

Greek women loved jewelry. They wore earrings, necklaces, armlets (worn above the elbow), bracelets, and anklets. Men wore rings as ornaments, some with gems in (except in Sparta, where they were made of plain iron). Children wore an amulet—a small piece of jewelry designed as a charm against evil. Many pieces of jewelry were made of gold and decorated with intricate designs.

Wool and weaving

Wool was the main fiber used for making clothes. First it was spun into yarn and dyed. Then the yarn was woven on stone-weighted looms (right) into very fine cloth, which hung beautifully when shaped into clothes. All of this work was done in the home by the women. Linen was also used. Coarse cloth was made from hemp, and the highest-quality garments were woven using luxurious silk from the island of Kos.

Index